A Note to Parents

DK READERS is a compelling program for beginning readers, designed in conjunction with leading literacy experts, including Dr. Linda Gambrell, Professor of Education at Clemson University. Dr. Gambrell has served as President of the National Reading Conference and the College Reading Association, and has been elected to serve as President of the International Reading Association.

Beautiful illustrations and superb full-color photographs combine with engaging, easy-to-read stories to offer a fresh approach to each subject in the series. Each DK READER is guaranteed to capture a child's interest while developing his or her reading skills, general knowledge, and love of reading.

The five levels of DK READERS are aimed at different reading abilities, enabling you to choose the books that are exactly right for your child:
Pre-level 1: Learning to read
Level 1: Beginning to read
Level 2: Beginning to read alone
Level 3: Reading alone
Level 4: Proficient readers

The "normal" age at which a child begins to read can be anywhere from three to eight years old, so these levels are intended only as a general guideline.

No matter which level you select, you can be sure that you are helping your child learn to read, then read to learn!

DK

LONDON, NEW YORK, MUNICH,
MELBOURNE, and DELHI

Produced by Southern Lights
Custom Publishing

For DK
Publisher Andrew Berkhut
Executive Editor Mary Atkinson
Art Director Tina Vaughan
Photographer Keith Harrelson

Reading Consultant
Linda Gambrell, Ph.D.

First American Edition, 2001
08 09 10 9 8 7 6 5 4 3
Published in the United States by DK Publishing
375 Hudson Street, New York, New York 10014

Library of Congress Cataloging-in-Publication Data
Hayward, Linda.
   Jobs people do. A day in the life of a musician / by Linda Hayward. --
1st American ed.
   p. cm. -- (DK readers)
   ISBN-13: 978-0-7894-7952-5 ISBN-10: 0-7894-7952-4 (plc) --
   ISBN-13: 978-0-7894-7953-2 ISBN-10: 0-7894-7953-2 (pb)
   1. Music-- Vocational guidance--Juvenile literature. [1. Musicians.
2. Occupations.] I. Title: Day in the life of a musician. II. Title. III.
Dorling Kindersley readers.

ML3795 .H39 2001
780'.23-dc21   2001028428

Color reproduction by Colourscan, Singapore
Printed and bound in China by L. Rex Printing Co., Ltd.

The characters and events in this story are fictional and do not represent real persons or events.
The publisher would like to thank the following
for their kind permission to reproduce their photographs:
Key: t=top, b=bottom, l=left, r=right, c=center
DK Picture Library: 5tr, 8t, 27c; Andy Crawford 4b, 21t; Phillip Dowell 19b; Steve Gorton 14bl;
Dave King 15br, 19tr, 19c; Tim Ridley 11tl. Howard L. Puckett 12t. The University of
Alabama at Birmingham: Steve Wood 22b. Models: Ay-Yi Bao, Chitra Desai, Emily Fleisig,
Glen Fleisig, Mary Jones, Kevin Kozak, Tariq Masri, Miles Parsons, June Pendergrass, Gerald
Rosenbaum, Lillian Sharp, Victoria Smith, Jo Ann Strickland, and Gracie Taylor.

In addition, Dorling Kindersley would like to thank the Alys Robinson Stephens Performing Arts
Center for use of the Jemison Concert Hall located on the campus of The University of Alabama
at Birmingham; Boutwell Studios, and Nuncie's Music Company for props and location
photography.

All other images © Dorling Kindersley Limited.
For further information see: www.dkimages.com

Discover more at
www.dk.com

DK READERS

BEGINNING
1
TO READ

A Day in the Life of a Musician

Written by Linda Hayward

DK Publishing

Jane Lee practices a tune
on her violin.

She will play
a solo
in a concert
tonight.

violin

Jane is a musician.

Jane's daughter, Emily, plays the flute.

flute

Emily's father claps when she finishes.

"You will have a good lesson today," he says.

Emily and her mother
go to the music store.
They look at sheet music
for Emily to play.

sheet
music

"Here is a tune
we can play together!"
says Jane.

"Can we look
at the instruments?" asks Emily.
"I want to play them all!"

"I could be
a drummer
in a rock band...

8

or play
the trumpet
and march
in a parade."

"The double bass
looks like a big violin!
It's bigger
than I am!

"I like to hear
the cymbals crash,"
says Emily.

"Come on,
it's time
to go,"
says Jane.

Jane takes Emily
to the music teacher's house.

"Dad will pick you up," says Jane.
"I have a recording session now."

Jane goes to the recording studio.
She will play music
for a TV commercial.

Two other musicians are already
at the recording studio.

Joey plays his guitar
to test the microphone.

microphone

Doug sets up his keyboard.
Now Joey and Doug are ready
to record the music.

Jane puts on headphones.
She is ready to play.
But where is Jamie,
the drummer?

headphones

Here comes Jamie.

"I had car trouble," he says.

Now they can record the music.

Emily's father picks her up
after her lesson.
"What did you
do today?"
he asks.

"I played a new tune," says Emily.
"Then my teacher
showed me instruments
from all over the world.

"She has
castanets
from Spain,

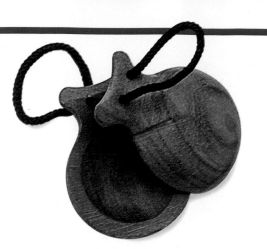

a sitar
from India,

and
a drum
from Africa."

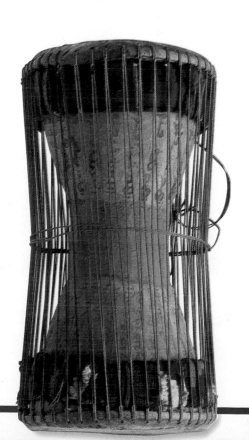

Emily and her father go home
and get dinner ready.

Jane is home just in time to eat!

After dinner, Jane hurries
to get ready for the concert.
She packs her music
and checks her bow.

bow

"Hurry, Mom," says Emily.
"Your ride is waiting outside."

Some of the other musicians are already at the concert hall.

concert
hall

Sam plays
the French horn.

Louise plays
the cello.

Andy plays
the bassoon.

Oh, no! Jane has
the wrong sheet music!

There is Emily backstage.
What is she doing there?
She has found Jane's sheet music!
It was mixed up
with her own music.

"You came just in time,"
says Jane.
"The conductor will
be ready soon."

The conductor will show
the musicians when to start
each piece of music.

He raises
his baton
to begin
the concert.

baton

The music starts.
Jane plays a beautiful solo.

Emily and her father listen
from the front row.

After the concert, they find Jane.

"I loved the music," says Emily.

Jane smiles.

She has the best job in the world!

Picture Word List

violin

headphones

flute

bow

sheet music

concert hall

microphone

baton